Angus Cleans Up

Written by Jenny Feely

Illustrated by Chantal Stewart

Flying Start
to Literacy®

T0363469

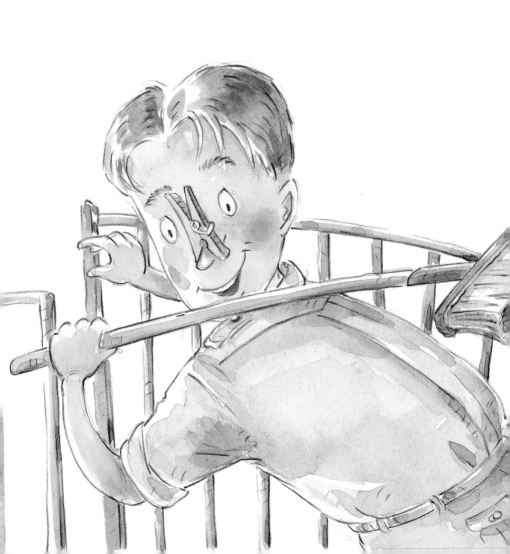

Contents

Chapter 1:
The new zookeeper

Angus was very excited when he became the new zookeeper.

"This zoo is smelly," he said to himself.
"I will make this zoo very clean.
A clean zoo is a happy zoo."

Angus started to work. He cleaned the elephant's pen. The elephant was very happy.

When he cleaned the monkeys' pen, they were very pleased too.

Then Angus went into the fox's pen.
The fox's pen looked clean but Angus
could smell a very strong smell.

"Don't get upset," said Angus to the fox.
"I will soon get rid of this smell."

And that is exactly what he did.

Chapter 2:
No more smells

Angus scrubbed and scrubbed and
scrubbed until the fox's pen
smelled fresh and clean.

But the fox was not happy because
it had put its smell around
to protect its hunting ground.
The fox bit Angus.

At the hyenas' pen, it was the same. There were more smells.

"Not to worry," said Angus as he got out his scrubbing brush.

Scrub, scrub, scrub went Angus.

"I bet you are happy now," said Angus.

But the hyenas were not happy. Their smell had protected their hunting ground.

Hyenas mark their territory with a strong smell.

Next Angus went to see the musk ox.

The musk ox was looking for a mate, so it was very smelly.

"Don't worry," said Angus. "I'll soon fix that."

Scrub, scrub, scrub went Angus.
Soon the musk ox was
as clean as could be
and it had lost its strong smell.

"Now you will be happy," said Angus.

But the musk ox was not happy.
It had made itself smelly because
it wanted to find a mate.
It looked very sad indeed.

But Angus didn't notice.

might think
ell bad but
ell very good
a lady ox.

Chapter 3:
Trouble for Angus

When Angus got to the skunk's pen, it was very smelly.

"Don't get upset," he said. "I will have you smelling good very soon."

He bent down to pick up the skunk.

When the skunk saw the scrubbing brush, it got so frightened it lifted its tail and sprayed Angus with a bad smell – a very, very bad smell.

Angus sniffed. He turned very pale and dropped his scrubbing brush.

"Ahhhh!" yelled Angus.

Angus scrubbed and scrubbed and scrubbed himself. But he could not get rid of that smell.

Chapter 4:
A smelly, happy zoo!

Angus was smelly for a very, very long time.

The boss of the zoo talked to Angus. "The animals may smell bad to you," he said. "But the animals need to smell this way because it helps them to be safe and to find a mate."

From then on, Angus let the animals keep their smells when he cleaned their pens.

The animals were happy and Angus was happy, too.

A note from the author

I have a very sensitive nose. Whenever a bad smell comes my way, you'll see me running for the cleaning products and throwing open all the windows. So when I was researching how animals use smell for my book *Animal Smells*, I kept thinking that it was just as well that I didn't have to get too close to these animals. I realized that I could never work in a zoo, looking after these animals. But what if I did? Would I try to get rid of the animals' smells? And that's when I got the idea for *Angus Cleans Up.*